Tennessee

A PHOTOGRAPHIC PORTRAIT

First published in the United States
of America by:

Twin Lights Publishers, Inc.
10 Hale Street
Rockport, Massachusetts 01966
Telephone: (978) 546-7398
http://www.twinlightspub.com

and

Yourtown Books
568 Ninth Street South
Suite 357
Naples, FL 34102
Telephone: (239) 633-6934

ISBN 1-88535-52-5

10 9 8 7 6 5 4 3 2 1

(right)

BYRON JORJORIAN

Cover photo by:
Byron Jorjorian

Editorial by:
Sarah FK Coble

Book design by
SYP Design & Production, Inc.
http://www.sypdesign.com

Printed in China

Memphis and West Tennessee   6

Central Tennessee   52

East Tennessee   90

Introduction

Tennessee: The name comes from *Tanasi,* the Cherokee word for the region around the Tennessee River. Slicing east to west from the Appalachian Mountains to the Mississippi River, the state of Tennessee, by its very location, is at the heart of America.

And yet, Tennessee is not easily defined by geography alone. Its landscape is so widely varied it has been called "three separate states within common boundaries," for the natural divisions that divide not only the landscape, but the cultural, political, and temperate climate as well.

Tennessee's "Grand Divisions" are defined by three major areas. The upland East, with its rugged slopes and ravines settled by the flinty natives who carved a living from the rocky soil in the mountains and valleys. Central Tennessee, all rolling hills and rich basins, made up of elegant horse farms and sleek cities. And the broad, lowlands and bluffs of Western Tennessee's delta region where cotton, the blues and rock 'n' roll are still king, marks the third.

Tennessee's history too, encompasses the greater story of the American nation in all its restless, adventuresome, and headstrong spirit.

For centuries, Cherokees, Chickasaws, Shawnees, and Creeks had claimed their living from the rich, hardwood forests, fertile plains host to herds of buffalo, elk, and deer, and mountain streams and quiet marshes of fish and other game. They moved west as European settlers broached the captivating and fearsome wilderness of the Tennessee frontier.

American politics, patriotism, and sense of place have deep roots in the Volunteer State. Before it took its place as the 16th state in 1796, it declared itself the sovereign nation of "Frankland" by the impatient, irascible pioneers that had settled the region. They were noted with alarm by the Governor of Louisiana as "adventurous and hostile to all subjection."

Yet, Tennesseans gained a reputation for volunteerism when great numbers re-crossed the mountains to fight for independence, a name that has stuck for two centuries. It was the last to secede from the Union in 1861, and yet it gave much to the Confederate cause and lost much. Yet, it always springs back. It is a state that perennially pulls itself up by its proverbial bootstraps.

With it all, Tennessee is the birthplace of American music, from the mountain music of the first pioneers to the country music of modern day Nashville, to the Blues and Soul that still rock the gritty heart of Memphis, music is the pulse of Tennessee.

Tennessee: A Photographic Portrait reveals a new view of this state of the American heart.

Greeter Falls

BYRON JORJORIAN

A wispy veil of water spills down the striated rocks of Savage Gulf State Natural Area. Eleven thousand five hundred acres of rocky gorges, cliffs, and streams, Savage Gulf's wilderness seems a world away.

Memphis and West Tennessee

Still Singing, But Not Just Singing the Blues: That's Memphis

It is true what that wise man said. You can't put your foot in the same river twice. The water keeps flowing to the sea: new water, new mud, new life, a new river every moment. So, when you find yourself in a place where a whole lot of rivers come together, you never know what will happen. That's Memphis.

The Mississippi Delta is the cradle of the Blues, and the Mississippi Delta begins in Memphis. It's the beginning of the end of that great muddy river rambling south to the sea. Years ago, steamboats carried just about everything and everyone north and south along that river, all passing through Memphis. The other side of the river is where the American west begins. So, Memphis was also a place where you crossed over going east and west: young men and mule trains heading west to find something better, tired old men heading back east if they didn't. Rivers of people carrying everything they needed, their own stories, their own songs, all passing through, looking for new beginnings. And right at the place where those rivers met, all the stories and songs and lives mixed together and started something else. The steamboats and the mules may be long gone, but the rivers still flow. Always bringing something new. That's Memphis.

When I went to Memphis as a boy from the farm down in Mississippi, I went to the big city to play the Blues. A young man could make his name playing the Blues in Memphis in the 1940's and many, many of us did. But the Memphis Blues started other American music and other names. Rock 'n' Roll and Soul found their beginnings in Memphis, too. You start singing one song and it becomes something new every time. Still singing, but not just the Blues anymore. That's Memphis.

The great, muddy Mississippi River keeps flowing, the highways keep going east and west, north and south, flowing through Memphis. There's always a new story, new music, new life. You keep sticking your foot in rivers and you'll always hit something new. That's Memphis.

—B.B. King

(above)

**Happy with
the Blues**

BOB GUTHRIDGE

The man himself
plays at B.B. King's
Blues Club, Beale
Street and Second.
B.B. King's distinctive
sound helped form
Memphis' place in
American music.

(pages 6-7)

**Southern Cypress
Reflection on
Powell Lake**

BYRON JORJORIAN

The lowland forests
of Tennessee provide
quiet havens for a
wide variety of plant
and animal life,
including beavers,
eagles, and the fox
squirrel.

Tree Frog
BYRON JORJORIAN

An unusual variety of the green tree (*Hyla Cinerea*) frog clings to leaves at Reelfoot Lake State Park.

(opposite)

Bottomland
BYRON JORJORIAN

Hardwood forests in the bottomlands along the Wolf River don't mind getting their feet wet. In segments of the Western Tennessee plains, where low-lying areas are saturated with backwaters and seepage from the rivers that feed into the Mississippi, bald cypress is a hard wood that flourishes in still waters.

Reflections on a Pond

BYRON JORJORIAN

The peaceful water of Travis-McNatt Lake at Big Hill Pond State Rustic Park 70 miles east of Memphis have a gem-like quality in this 4,500-acre natural area that encompasses lakes, rivers, meadows, hills and swamps. Once occupied by the Chickasaw tribe, visitors can still see evidence of an old Indian settlement in the park.

(opposite)

Water Lotus – Cypress Knees

BYRON JORJORIAN

The average depth of Reelfoot is only 5.5 feet deep, barely covering the old forest that stood before the earthquake. The tangle of fallen hardwood trees beneath the water's surface has created one of the world's premiere natural fish hatcheries with more than 55 species of fish.

**Wintering at Reelfoot
Lake State Park**
BYRON JORJORIAN

A mature bald eagle
commands a winter
bare branch at
Reelfoot State Park in
the heart of
Tennessee delta
country. The region
was a favorite nesting
ground for American
bald eagles, but
ended in 1963.
Tennessee began
reintroducing young
eagles to the area in
1980. Ten years later,
nearly 250 eagles
return to Reelfoot for
the winter.

(below)

Canoe on Kelso Lake
BYRON JORJORIAN

25 million acres of
oak and cypress
swamp forest domi-
nated the landscape
when the first white
settlers arrived in
western Tennessee.
Hatchie National
Wildlife Refuge pre-
serves over 9,400
acres of prime bot-
tomland forest that
provide breeding
habitat for numerous
migratory waterfowl
and mammals.

(opposite)

Sentinel
BYRON JORJORIAN

A great horned owl
peers out of his niche
at Reelfoot National
Wildlife Refuge.
Eagles, hawks, and
many types of owls
and other birds of
prey have put
Reelfoot on the list
of Globally Important
Bird Areas.

(right)

**Cypress Knees,
Reelfoot Lake State
Park**
BYRON JORJORIAN

Bald Cypress
(Taxodium distichum)
is native to North
America and once
dominated swamps
of the Southeastern
U.S. Bald Cypress
sends up woody
growths or "knees"
from their roots,
which is believed to
provide the swamp-
dwelling tree with
adequate oxygen.

(below)

**Lee House,
Victorian Village**
MONTY S. JOHNSON

Mid-19th century
Memphis wealth pro-
duced a number of
palatial homes built
on the quiet outskirts
of the city. Now part
of the city's downtown
district, "Victorian
Village" is a leafy walk
through Memphis'
gracious past.

(opposite)

**American Water
Lotus**
BYRON JORJORIAN

A flamboyant floral
display, the American
water lotus (*Nelumbo
Lutea*) grows in mas-
sive beds in quiet,
shallow waters of
North America. The
plate-sized flowers
produce large seed
capsules containing a
number of seeds that
were also known as
the Yackey nut or the
water chinquapin.
Roasted or ground
into a sweet, starchy
flour, these seeds
were a staple of the
Native American and
American pioneer
diet.

right)

10,000 Acres
BYRON JORJORIAN

Wetlands cover 90% of the Hatchie River region in Southwest Tennessee, the last unaltered river in the lower Mississippi River Valley. The Hatchie National Wildlife Refuge, 11,556 acres established in 1964, was established to conserve this virgin habitat for native and migratory waterbirds, other plant and animal life as well as a peaceful refuge for human visitors.

(opposite, top)

Cypress Summer Dress
BYRON JORJORIAN

Cypress and water lotus deck themselves out in summer finery at Reelfoot Lake State Park. Deciduous, bald cypress is so named to distinguish it from true, evergreen varieties.

(opposite, bottom)

Gold Lotus
BYRON JORJORIAN

Many old Tennessee families still harvest the seed pods of the American water lotus to make flour for special holiday cakes.

**Burrow Library,
Rhodes College**

ERNIE PICK

Burrow Library
reflects the ideals of
an atmosphere of
learning set in a
Christian frame of
reference for this
small idyllic college
in Southwest
Memphis.

Rhodes Gothic

ERNIE PICK

Founded in 1848, the
campus of Rhodes
College was built on
a philosophy that a
learning environment
enhances personal
connections and iden-
tity can positively
effect education.
This ideology per-
vades Rhodes'
Oxford-like setting in
Memphis. Now, 13
Collegiate Gothic
style buildings on the
campus are listed on
the National Register
of Historic Places.

(right)

Memphis Queen
COURTESY OF MEMPHIS
CONVENTION AND
VISITOR'S BUREAU

Memphis' position at the confluence of the Wolf and Mississippi Rivers made the city an important river port for shipping cotton, timber, travelers and settlers. The grand riverboats also brought itinerant jazz musicians and other entertainers to the city that would eventually become a hub of uniquely American music.

(below)

Tennessee River Pearl
BYRON JORJORIAN

The Tennessee State gem is the Tennessee River Pearl, the glimmering baroque pearls from freshwater mussels. On the banks of the Mighty Mississippi, the lights of Memphis glimmer like baroque gems of the state.

(above)

Going to Graceland
BYRON JORJORIAN

Elvis' beloved Graceland opened to the public in 1982. As one of the most visited homes in America, it laid the cornerstone to Memphis' tourism industry, spawning other attractions such as the National Civil Rights Museum, Rock and Soul Museum, the Gibson Guitar Factory and the World Championship Barbecue Cooking Contest.

(right)

**Made from Cotton:
Mallory-Neely House**
BOB GUTHRIDGE

The 25-room,
Italianate house at
652 Adams Avenue in
the Victorian Village
Historic District was
the residence of well-
to-do 19th century
cotton factors and
merchants, James C.
Neely and Barton Lee
Mallory families. It is
still filled with many
of the families' fur-
nishings, including
Chinese pieces
bought at the
Louisiana Purchase
Exposition of 1903.

(opposite)

James Lee House
BOB GUTHRIDGE

The base of this
Italianate fantasy was
built in 1848 with the
second story added
on in the 1860's.
Clustered together in
the neighborhood
north of Memphis'
downtown, many of
the structures in
Victorian Village were
rescued from bull-
dozers in the 1970's.

The Pink Palace

Clarence Saunders, founder of Piggly Wiggly foodstore chain had great plans in the early 1920's for his mansion of pink Georgian marble. Bankrupt in the late 1920's however, he turned it over to the city. "The Pink Palace" headquarters the Pink Palace Family of Museums, including Coon Creek Science Center, Sharpe Planetarium, Lichterman Nature Center, the Mallory-Neely and Magevney Houses as well as an IMAX theater.

(opposite)

Civil Courthouse, Memphis
ERNIE PICK

Architect James Gamble Rogers designed the Neoclassical Revival structure of the Shelby County Courthouse in 1905 and is an imposing, impressive building that occupies an entire block in the center of downtown Memphis. Originally dedicated in 1910, the building, which was renovated from 1980 to1992, is now listed on the National Historic Register.

Zoo Avenue

COURTESY OF MEMPHIS
CONVENTION AND
VISITOR'S BUREAU

Stone silhouettes guard
the entrance to the
Memphis Zoo which
takes its inspiration
from the city's Egyptian
namesake. Visitors
enter into 70 acres of
pleasant botanical
walkways and other
artistically created
animal habitats.

The Great Pyramids at Memphis
ERNIE PICK

A 20-foot tall statue of Ramesses the Great presides over the entrance to The Pyramid, the stainless steel and glass nod to the city's namesake Memphis, Egypt. The 32-story, sports and entertainment arena underwent an identity crisis when the NBA team, the Memphis Grizzlies, moved into a new facility. The Memphis City Council voted to keep the 22,500-seat sports arena open.

RAMESSE
THE GREA

China at the Memphis Zoo

STEVEN MORGAN

This exotic pavilion is a grand entrance to the China exhibit at the Memphis Zoo. This exhibit is a tribute to the country's history, culture and plant life as well as its animal life. The China exhibit is one of many "inclusive habitats" created by the Memphis Zoo since the 1990's. After many years of negotiations with China, two giant pandas, Ya Ya and Le Le, arrived at the Memphis Zoo in the Spring of 2003. These rare creatures had previously only been on exhibit at the zoos of Atlanta, San Diego, and Washington, D.C.

(opposite)

Silhouettes at Sunset

BYRON JORJORIAN

Bald cypress was an important commodity in the Southern U.S., where it grew abundantly in low-lying swampy areas such as the delta region of Tennessee.

Father of Waters
COURTESY OF MEMPHIS
CONVENTION AND
VISITOR'S BUREAU

Lights of downtown
Memphis sparkle on
the waters of the
mighty Mississippi.
Originally a Chickasaw
Indian village, the city
on the Mississippi
delta was named for
the ancient Egyptian
city on the Nile delta.
It is now the busiest
commercial and trans-
portation hub of the
South, and, largely
due to the great river
at its doorstep, still
one of the largest cot-
ton and lumber mar-
kets in the world.

(below)

Urban Blues
COURTESY OF MEMPHIS
CONVENTION AND
VISITOR'S BUREAU

In the 1920's
Memphis' steamy
nightlife was a Mecca
for a new breed of
musicians playing the
Blues. Musical legends
like Howlin' Wolf,
Muddy Waters, and
B.B. King came to
Memphis and rocked
the cradle of music
that would later
inspire Soul, Jazz
and Rock 'n' Roll.

(opposite)

Memphis-Arkansas
THOMAS "HANK" HOGAN

Also known as "Old
Bridge," the Memphis-
Arkansas Bridge was
opened in 1949, the
third bridge to cross
the Mississippi at
Memphis. Often
described as "long,
strong, and ugly," the
Memphis-Arkansas is
still a major trucking
route, but now seems
dwarfed by the new
Hernando De Soto,
which opened in 1973.

In the AutoZone
ERNIE PICK

Memphians flock to
the AutoZone base-
ball stadium to sup-
port their hometeam,
the Class AAA
Redbirds.

**Just Like Elvis'
Mama Used to Make**
ERNIE PICK

Elvis Presley's
Memphis on Beale
Street features many
of his mother Gladys'
recipes and many of
"The King's" favorite
dishes. Sorry, fried
banana sandwiches
are not on the menu.

(right)

Memphis Concierge
KANDIE STREFLING
FIRST PLACE, MEMPHIS

A mustachioed feline welcomes visitors to this friendly front porch in the Historic District in Memphis. Although it is a bustling city, Memphis' easy-going attitude permeates every aspect of urban life.

(below)

Gibson Guitar Factory
ERNIE PICK
THIRD PLACE, MEMPHIS

Guitars are still made by hand at the Gibson Guitar Factory in downtown Memphis. The venerable factory shares its location on Lt. George W. Lee Avenue with the Smithsonian's Rock 'n' Soul museum.

(opposite)

182 Beale Street
GARY KESSEL
SECOND PLACE, MEMPHIS

Barrelhouse, Boogie and the Blues, the Rum Boogie Café is one of Beale Street's most famous night spots.

Keepers of the Flame
COURTESY OF MEMPHIS
CONVENTION AND
VISITOR'S BUREAU

Memphis' slow-
cooked barbecue is
legendary. In May
1978, 20 teams of
barbecue enthusiasts
cooked their finest
for $1,000 in cash
prizes and all the
pork shoulder and
ribs they could eat.
Now, over 225 teams
compete for the
ultimate title in the
*Memphis in May
World Championship
Barbecue Cooking
Contest.*

(opposite)

**If Beale Street
Could Talk**
THOMAS "HANK" HOGAN

Beale Street plays a
colorful role in
Memphis history and
its ongoing renova-
tion is testament to
Memphians tenacity
and pride in their
city. In the late
1970's the city pur-
chased nearly all of
the historic buildings
of Beale Street in an
effort to revive the
district. Since then,
Beale Street has
become a hot spot
again.

(right)

Elvis Has Left the Building

Elvis' legend lives on in Memphis, but his restaurant, Elvis Presley's Memphis will not. After nearly 6 years in operation at 126 Beale Street, the old Lansky Brothers' Store, Elvis Presley Enterprises closed its doors.

(below)

On Company Time

Many of the craftsmen at the Gibson Guitar Factory are musicians and though dedicated to the craft of creating the finest guitars in the world, on-the-job jam sessions are common.

(opposite)

Streetcar Named Desire

In 1993, Memphis Area Transit Authority opened a vintage trolley line to connect parts of downtown Memphis with other historic districts in the city. The success of the quaint, historic streetcars inspired the transit agency to expand trolley service to include a 2-mile riverfront loop and to create a master plan for light rail service for all of the Memphis metro area.

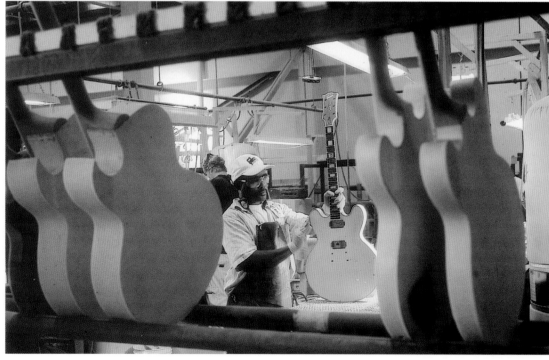

(right)

Elvis Presley Boulevard

ERNIE PICK

To say that Elvis is everything to the cradle of American music would be inaccurate. However, Elvis' Graceland Mansion at 3734 Elvis Presley Boulevard (formerly Highway 51 South) is Memphis' biggest attraction and one of the most visited houses in the country, second only to the White House.

(below)

Hard Rock and B.B. King's Blues Club

ERNIE PICK

Memphis' Hard Rock Café on Beale Street occupies a historic building that has been at various times a saloon and a recording studio. Now serving up traditional American fare to a funky beat, this international restaurant chain is at home in Memphis. When blues legend B.B. King came to Memphis in 1946 from Indianola, Mississippi to seek his fortune, Beale Street was still a hotbed of fast living and cool music. King opened his namesake club at 143 Beale Street in 1991, drawing tourists and locals alike.

(opposite)

Good Morning, Memphis

ERNIE PICK

This hard-boiled welcome to Memphis at the downtown visitors' center is a cheerful reminder of Memphis' rich cultural history.

(right)

Graceland

Elvis bought the mansion named for the previous owner, Grace Toof, on the outskirts of Memphis in 1957 for just over $100,000. He lived at Graceland until his death in 1977. Fans still make the pilgrimage to tour this national historic landmark, the 14-acre grounds, and gravesite.

(below)

Formal Room at Graceland

Far less flamboyant than the rest of the Graceland mansion, the living room at Graceland was where Elvis' funeral was held in August 1977.

(opposite)

At Home with the Presleys

Of the 16 television sets scattered throughout Graceland, three were mounted in the TV room so that the King could watch sporting events simultaneously. The chrome and glass room was also the central control for state-of-the-art media equipment.

(right)

Pink Cadillac
COURTESY OF MEMPHIS
CONVENTION AND
VISITORS BUREAU
AND GRACELAND

In addition to touring Graceland, visitors can climb aboard the *Lisa Marie,* one of the King's two private jets, and view his vintage car collection, including the famous 1955 pink Cadillac.

(below)

Hot Lap
COURTESY OF MEMPHIS
CONVENTION AND
VISITORS BUREAU

Memphis International Motorsport Park, located between Memphis and Millington, opened in 1986 as a multi-track facility. The facility now attracts NASCAR race participants and fans worldwide.

(below and opposite)

Peabody Duck March
COURTESY OF THE
PEABODY HOTEL

In the 1930's Frank Shutt, general manager of The Peabody Hotel, and friend Chip Barwick, returned from a hunting trip. After a few too many sips of Tennessee whiskey, they put three small ducks into the lobby's grand marble fountain, and a Memphis tradition was born. The Peabody Ducks have since become an international icon. Each morning four mallard ducks and their Duck Master parade the red carpet to the music of John Philip Sousa's *King Cotton March.* The pinnacle of Southern elegance in the 1920's and '30's, the hotel fell upon hard times in the 1960's and '70's. It was restored to its former grandeur in 1981. The duck tradition, however, went uninterrupted.

(left)

Bright Lights, Big City

COURTESY OF MEMPHIS CONVENTION AND VISITORS BUREAU

Lighting the way to Tennessee's largest city, lights on the Memphis-Arkansas bridge illuminate the sky over the dark, muddy waters of the Mississippi.

(opposite)

Walkin' in Memphis

COURTESY OF MEMPHIS CONVENTION AND VISITORS BUREAU

Named in 1841 after an obscure military hero, Beale Street was the headquarters for occupying Union forces during the Civil War. During the 1920's however, it was a lively place where pickpockets, prostitutes, and penny ante gamblers strolled side by side with blues kings and voodoo queens. The zoot suit was a Beale Street creation as was the hot snoot sandwich.

**Monkey See
Monkey Do**

THOMAS "HANK" HOGAN

A visitor to the
Memphis Zoo regards a
resident baboon. Other
state-of-the-art habi-
tats in this city favorite
are Cat Country,
Dragon's Lair, Primate
Canyon, a seasonal
butterfly house, a
19th-century farm,
and a lavish aquarium.

The Color of Money

KANDIE STREFLING

Tobacco has long been
one of Tennessee's top
commodities. Varieties
such as Burley, Dark
Fire Cured and Dark
Air Cured are grown
over approximately
59,000 acres, produc-
ing nearly 111 million
pounds worth over
$218 million annually.

Central Tennessee

(left)

Making Hay While the Sun Shines

BYRON JORJORIAN

Hay cures in the sunshine on a farm in Williamson County in Central Tennessee. Some of Tennessee's richest farmland is concentrated in this county not far from Nashville.

(below)

Echinacea Tennesseensis

BYRON JORJORIAN

A rare native of Tennessee's Cumberland Plateau, Tennessee's tenacious purple coneflower's long taproot winds through the rocky soil of the cedar glades of the region.

(opposite)

Scenic River Runs Wild

BYRON JORJORIAN

The Obed River and its two main tributaries, Clear Creek and Daddy's Creek, carve out some of the most ruggedly beautiful scenery in East Tennessee's Cumberland Plateau. The Obed's 45 miles of creeks and rapids were designated as a National Wild and Scenic River in 1976.

(pages 52-53)

Great Falls

BYRON JORJORIAN

The Great Falls on the Caney Fork River reign supreme at Rock Island State Park in Central Tennessee. Woodlands, lakes, gorges and waterfalls traverse this broad region west of the Tennessee River that comprises much of the state's central region.

(right)

Farm at Leiper's Fork

BYRON JORJORIAN

Now an idyllic farming area, Leiper's Fork was the site of a fierce battle in April 1863, in which Confederate troops routed a Federal attack. Nearly 1600 American soldiers fell on these peaceful fields and pastures.

(below)

Cattle at Thompson Station

BYRON JORJORIAN

Bluegrass grows over much of Tennessee's Central Basin, which makes the middle part of the state rich grazing land for its many magnificent horse and cattle farms. The sale of cattle was the leading source of farm income in the late 1990's, but it is horses, most notably, the distinctive Tennessee Walking Horse, that bears the state's name.

(opposite)

When the Frost is on the Pumpkin, Franklin, Tennessee

BYRON JORJORIAN

Central Tennessee's farming base is diverse, with cash crops of cotton, soybeans, tobacco, corn and other plants. However, in 2001, Tennessee showed a rapid increase in pumpkin farming and "Agritainment" farming. Tennessee's numerous small farms are prime places for fall farm activities such as apple picking, hay rides and picking your own Halloween pumpkin.

Image used with permission of Gentry's Farm.

Stone Door

BYRON JORJORIAN

Carved into the rocks of the Cumberland Plateau, the Savage Gulf State Natural Area is a system of steep cliffs, dramatic canyons and creeks that tumble down rugged gorges. Stone Door, only 10 feet wide but 100 feet deep was used by native tribes as a passage from the plateau above to the gorges below.

Nesting at Radnor Lake

BYRON JORJORIAN

Migrating birds discovered 85-acre Radnor Lake soon after its construction in 1914 as a reservoir for the Louisville-Nashville Railroad and livestock at Radnor Yards. At the request of the Tennessee Ornithological Society in 1923, L&N prohibited hunting, declaring the lake a wildlife sanctuary. In 1973 the man-made lake was made Tennessee's first official state natural area.

Greeter Falls, Savage Gulf

BYRON JORJORIAN

Cold, quick streams meander through hardwood forests of oak, hickory, maple and poplar and drop into breathtaking waterfalls. Greeter Falls pitches over a 15-foot upper caprock before plummeting over a 50-foot ledge below.

**Across the
Great Divide**

BYRON JORJORIAN

Cades Cove, an 11-mile hiking loop in the Great Smoky Mountain National Park, follows the old wagon trails used by Tennessee's first settlers. The beloved national park preserves native plant and animal life, providing visitors with a view much the same as the ones seen by the first European settlers as they crossed the Great Divide.

State Wildflower

BYRON JORJORIAN

The passionflower
(Passiflora incarnata)
was chosen in 1919
by Tennessee school-
children as the state
wildflower. Also
called the maypop,
the wild apricot and
the ocoee, passiflora
incarnata is an excep-
tional variety of the
400 or more species
of passionflowers in
its hardiness to cold
weather. Native tribes
prized the ocoee
flower for its abun-
dant beauty, as well
as for its herbal and
healing properties.

(below)

Rivers Under Glass

ERNIE PICK

THIRD PLACE, NASHVILLE

A river runs through
the Delta Atrium at
Gaylord Opryland
Hotel. Over a quarter
mile long, the Delta
was christened in
1996 with the
"Blending of the
Waters," a ceremony
into which water from
rivers around the
world were poured

(opposite)

Winter Sunrise

BYRON JORJORIAN

In the southern sec-
tion of Nashville
itself, Radnor Lake is
Tennessee's most vis-
ited natural area.
Easily accessible to
urban residents, the
1,100-acre watershed
ecosystem of wooded
hills, high limestone
hills, streams, and
the deep lake, Radnor
teems with native
plant and animal life.
In winter, it is home
to 23 species of
migratory birds.

(right)

Duck River

BYRON JORJORIAN

The Duck River has more than 20 miles of waterway for exploration. The area is a prime location to watch wildlife and birds such as kingfishers, herons, ospreys and other birds of prey, and—yes—ducks.

(opposite, top)

Rock Island, Still Water

BYRON JORJORIAN

In December of 1863, Rock Island became the site of a prison camp for Confederate soldiers after the Battle of Lookout Mountain. The last prisoners were released in June, 1865. In 1969, Rock Island was made a state park, letting the waters of the Caney Fork and Collins Rivers wash over old wounds.

(opposite, bottom)

Guarding the Past

BYRON JORJORIAN

The area surrounding Thompson Station is one of Tennessee's fastest growing, yet it still retains its distinctive rural charm and historic pride. During the battle of Thompson Station, 17-year old Alice Thompson dashed into the street to retrieve the colors of the 3rd Arkansas Regiment when the flagbearer fell. Her rash act of courage inspired the Confederates to win the battle.

(above)

Agriculture and Commerce— Tennessee State Motto

STEVEN SCHMOLDT
SECOND PLACE, NASHVILLE

The former estate of native Tennessee tycoon, Rogers Caldwell, was modeled after the Hermitage, the house of Tennessee's other famous son and the country's 7th president, Andrew Jackson. The 207-acre farmland just south of Nashville now houses the Tennessee Department of Agriculture, Tennessee Wildlife Resources Agency and other government agencies.

(below)

Welcome to Dollywood

BYRON JORJORIAN

In 1986, a small attraction in Pigeon Forge paired with an Eastern Tennessee country superstar and Dollywood was born. Blending an ever-changing vista of entertainment and "homespun fun," including attractions such as "Back Porch Theater" and the old steam locomotive, "Klondike Katie," this is a little theme park that could.

(opposite)

Brentwood

BYRON JORJORIAN

Yellow flowers blaze in a quiet spot in Brentwood, near Nashville. In the late 1700's, land around Brentwood was granted by the state of North Carolina to veterans of the Revolutionary War. By the time of the Civil War in 1861, the fertile region was the richest in the state.

(left and right)

Gaylord Opryland Resort and Convention Center, Nashville

ERNIE PICK

The Opryland Hotel, on the outskirts of Nashville, envelops 9 acres in glass to create an indoor rainforest fantasia.

Cascading waterfalls, pools and streams meander between 50,000 different plants throughout three separate courtyards.

(above)

**Gaylord Opryland
Resort and
Convention Center,
Nashville**
BYRON JORJORIAN

Outside, Opryland
Hotel may seem like
simple ol' Southern
hospitality, but
inside, the destination
hotel outside
Nashville will knock
your socks off with
resident cascading
waterfalls, babbling
brooks and fountains
that dance with state-
of-the-art lights and
lasers.

(below)

**Grand Ole Opry
House**
BYRON JORJORIAN

In 1972, Tennessee's
world-famous Grand
Ole Opry moved out
to the suburbs. It's
home is now officially
"Opryland," located in
Music Valley, a sub-
urb of Nashville. The
nearby Opryland
Theme Park closed in
1997 to re-open as an
outlet mall.

(right)

Parthenon

CHARLES F. REIST

After its debut at the Tennessee Centennial Exposition in 1897, the Parthenon, the full-scale replica of the Athens original stood as a grand centerpiece to the empty fairgrounds. In 1902, Centennial Park became the largest city park in Nashville. Intended as a temporary architectural fantasy, the structure was fully restored from 1991-2001.

(below)

Wildhorses

GAYLORD OPRYLAND
RESORT AND
CONVENTION CENTER

Once a historic warehouse in Nashville, The Wildhorse Saloon's three levels host the hottest live country music and the best boot-scootin' in Central Tennessee. To kick off the grand opening in 1994, the Wildhorse celebrated with a cattle stampede right past its doors on Second Avenue.

(opposite)

Old Hickory's Hermitage

MINDY SCHWARTZ

In 1804, Andrew Jackson bought the first 425 acres near Nashville that would become the site of his beloved Hermitage, a graceful, two-story, Greek Revival-style mansion that visitors see today. Jackson and his wife Rachel, however, lived in a modest cabin for 17 years before commissioning the house in 1819.

(right)

How-deeee!

BYRON JORJORIAN

The historic Ryman Auditorium in downtown Nashville hosted classical greats such as actress Sarah Bernhardt, opera great Enrico Caruso and composer John Philip Sousa. Yet it is most famous as the original stage of Tennessee's famous Grand Ole Opry starting the careers of country music icons, like Loretta Lynn, Hank Williams, and Minnie Pearl.

(below)

The Bandwagon

BYRON JORJORIAN

"The Grand Opera" was broadcast by a small Nashville radio station in 1925 and quickly became known in the local dialect as "The Grand Ole Opry." The chance to perform on the stage of the Ryman Auditorium drew country musicians to Nashville and local record producers sprang up, earning the city the nickname "Music City."

(opposite)

The Modern Look of Country Music

BYRON JORJORIAN

Nashville's modern skyline provides a sleek backdrop to the old brick exterior of the historic Ryman Auditorium. For years, major record producers ignored Nashville's "hillbilly" music. Local producers began their own recordings of country's distinctive sounds. Today, nearly every major commercial producer has an office and recording facility in Nashville.

Captain Ryman Sees the Future

BYRON JORJORIAN

Captain Tom Ryman was a steamboat captain in late 19th century Nashville, notorious for his hard drinking, and fast living. In 1892, Captain Ryman found God, changed his wicked ways, and built The Union Gospel Tabernacle near Nashville's hard luck Black Bottoms District. After his death in 1904, the community re-named the theater in his honor.

(below)

The Spirit of Captain Tom Ryman

BYRON JORJORIAN

The Ryman Auditorium has become woven into the fabric of Nashville's past and present. Many Nashvillians claim that Ryman's spirit still haunts the old Tabernacle on 5th Avenue in Nashville, expressing his disapproval for shows that don't meet his standards.

(opposite)

Ryman Auditorium

BYRON JORJORIAN

Thomas Ryman built his turn-of-the-century church for approximately $130,000. From 1992 to 1994, nearly 20 years after the Grand Ole Opry had left the building, the Ryman Auditorium was restored and re-opened for $8.5 million. Declared to have better acoustics than Carnegie Hall, the Ryman has been regularly voted to be one of the best venues for live music in the nation.

Reflecting on the Future
KHENA KARA

(right)

Nashville's place in American history is unique, but it also looks to a vibrant future. In addition to its signature music industry, Nashville is home to a number of Fortune 500 companies, such as telecommunications titan, Bell South.

(opposite)

Titans of Tennessee
KHENA KARA

Since 1999, the Adelphia Coliseum in Nashville has been the home of the Tennessee Titans football team. Formerly the Houston Oilers, the team moved in 1997 to the Liberty Bowl Memorial Stadium in Memphis, naming themselves after the Greek Giants of power, strength and knowledge.

(right)

Rollin' on the River
BYRON JORJORIAN

The *General Jackson* illuminates the night on the Cumberland River as it flows past Opryland USA, where the Grand Ole Opry has lived since 1974. The 300-foot-long *General Jackson,* named after the original 1817 steamboat, follows the grand showboat tradition with Opry-style shows performed in the magnificent Victorian-style theater on the main deck.

(below)

Southern Bell Celebration
BYRON JORJORIAN

Fourth of July fireworks rocket past the Bell South Building and light up the Nashville skyline. A city already known for its glitter, Nashville's 20 year traditional Independence Day Firework Celebration at Riverfront Park is an all-out, booming extravaganza.

(opposite)

Fountains of Fire
RANDY LYNN BLEVINS

In a city already known for its stars and sequins, Nashville lights up the night with a celebration of fireworks on the river.

(right)

Tennessee Foxtrot Carousel, Gazelle and Tiger

ANNE B. BOND

Located at Riverfront Park in Nashville, this whimsical merry-go-round features three-dimensional and paintings of Nashville native, Red Grooms. The runner pictured, Wilma Rudolph, also a Tennessee native who astounded the world as a gold medallist in the 1956 Olympics, was admiringly known as the "Black Gazelle."

(below)

Grand Ole Opry

GAYLORD OPRYLAND RESORT AND CONVENTION CENTER

The Possum Hunters were the first country band to play on WSM radio in the 1920's, the call letters that would soon be Nashville's voice to the world. Now staged in the 4,400 seat Grand Ole Opry House in Opryland, fans can also listen in live via satellite networks and opry.com.

(opposite)

Toot-Toot Tootsie, Goodbye.

ANNE B. BOND

Operated by the late, great Tootsie Bess, Tootsie's Orchid Lounge on Broadway in Nashville is a luridly painted honky tonk with a heart of gold. Just across the alley from the Ryman Auditorium, Tootsie's became the waiting room for Opry performers such as Patsy Kline, Hank Cochran, and Waylon Jennings. The ghost of Hank Williams still regularly performs here.

(above)

Night Light
RANDY LYNN BLEVINS
FIRST PLACE, NASHVILLE

Lightning from a summer storm strikes down on the highest towers of the Bell South Building, known affectionately as "The Batman Building." Built in 1994, it is one of the most distinguished structures of Nashville's urban skyline.

(above)

Capitol Christmas
LOUISA AVERY

Noted architect
William Strickland
died during construc-
tion of what he con-
sidered his greatest
achievement, the
Tennessee State
Capitol building. He
was buried on the
north side in 1854.
The building's corner-
stone was laid in 1845
and was completed in
1859. It is also the
site of the tombs of
former President and
Mrs. James Polk.

Hall of Fame
COURTESY OF COUNTRY
MUSIC HALL OF FAME

A Tennessee institution since 1967, the Country Music Hall of Fame and Museum dedicated its $37 million landmark building on the west bank of the Cumberland River in May 2001. Located in the entertainment district near the historic Ryman Auditorium, the distinctive museum keeps a vast collection of this trademark American art form.

(below)

Customs House
ERNIE PICK

This ornate, beautifully appointed building has been one of Tennessee's best examples of Victorian architecture. Until the late 20th century this building was owned by the United States Government. With the help of the Nashville Metropolitan Government which took possession of this building, it now can be preserved and redeveloped for future generations.

(opposite)

Greenway Bridge
STEVEN P. SCHMOLDT

A bankrupt amusement park was purchased by Nashville's park board and opened to the public on July 4th, 1912, making Shelby Park the oldest park in the city. Now a favorite urban spot for birders, runners and ballplayers, Shelby Bottoms became part of the Nashville Metro Greenway system in 1997.

(right

Façade of a National Treasure
BYRON JORJORIAN

"If I could pick one structure that truly embodies our country's music heritage, it would have to be the Ryman Auditorium" —Congressman Bob Clement. In June 2001, the Ryman Auditorium was named a National Historic Landmark. There are approximately 2,330 Historic Landmarks listed on the National Register, the official list of cultural and historic properties worthy of preservation.

(below)

Over Downtown Nashville
BYRON JORJORIAN

Ancient tribes built mounds at the site on the Cumberland River bluffs centuries before the first Europeans established Fort Nashborough in 1779. Daniel Boone brought white settlers over the Appalachians on the Wilderness Road. The population grew quickly and as soon as 1806 it was chartered. It became Tennessee's state capital in 1843.

(opposite)

On the Trail of the Natchez Trace
LOUISA AVERY

For 440 miles, this historic National Scenic Trail passes Indian mounds, cypress bottomlands and gentle southern landscape from Natchez, Mississippi to Nashville, Tennessee. For centuries it served as a trading route for native tribes, government officials and fortune seekers.

(right)

Hitching a Ride on a Riverboat Queen

BYRON JORJORIAN

The golden age of riverboats was the mid-19th century and Nashville prospered from the raucous steam-powered riverboats that churned up and down the Cumberland River carrying manufactured goods, commodities, and people to the bustling capital city.

(below)

Showboating

COURTESY OF GAYLORD OPRYLAND RESORT AND CONVENTION CENTER

Robert Fulton harnessed steam power for water travel in 1807 and ushered in the romantic era of the American riverboat. These multi-tiered wedding cake boats inspired the dreams of many young men to pilot these broad-bottomed, multi-tiered vessels that chugged the Tennessee's broad rivers.

(opposite)

River Front

BYRON JORJORIAN

Steamboats were made obsolete by the advent of the modern railroad. The late 20th century opened a new age of tall stacks. Many of America's river cities, including Nashville, have revived the romantic era of the riverboat for entertainment and transportation. The *General Jackson,* a replica of a 19th-century riverboat, taxis passengers from Opryland USA to downtown Nashville several times a day.

East Tennessee

Before the Falls

BYRON JORJORIAN

A fly fisherman kneels at the water's edge of Abrams Falls, a 20-foot cascade in the Great Smoky Mountain National Park. Named for a local Cherokee chief, Abrams Falls is a favorite hike for many park visitors.

(below)

Seeking Shelter

BYRON JORJORIAN

The Big South Fork National River and Recreation Area is 106,000 acres of forest, canyons, rivers and sandstone arches that once sheltered Cherokee and Shawnee hunters. The depleted land was turned over to the National Park Service in 1989. Big South Fork's second growth forests are evidence of nature's resiliency.

(opposite)

Drive-Thru Nature Trail

BYRON JORJORIAN

Mountain streams, wild-flowers, and waterfalls can all be seen without leaving your car at Roaring Fork Motor Trail outside of Gatlin-burg in the Great Smoky Mountain National Park. A five-mile loop takes auto-hikers past historic Bud Ogle Farm, through scenic green forests.

(previous page)

Rolling Waters

BYRON JORJORIAN

Birch Branch Creek flows through the heart of the Cherokee National Forest in the rolling hills of eastern-most Tennessee. The 425-acre John R. Dickey Birch Branch Sanctuary was donated to the Tennessee chapter of The Nature Conser-vancy in 1996.

(right)

Lichens, Ferns, Rocks and Void

BYRON JORJORIAN

A quiet enclave of ferns and moss enchant visitors at Fall Creek Falls, a 17,000 acre state park on the Cumberland Plateau, near the dividing line between the central and eastern portions of Tennessee. In addition to its huge 250-foot falls, Fall Creek has some of the country's most beautiful caves full of extremely rare cave fauna.

(below)

Shimmering Grotto

BYRON JORJORIAN

Passing from the summit of Mount Le Conte, through a forest of hemlock, beeches, maples, silverbells and rhododendrons, the Roaring Fork Creek cascades 30 feet into the plunge pool of Grotto Falls in the Great Smoky Mountain National Park.

(opposite)

Listen to the Mockingbird

BYRON JORJORIAN

Tennessee's state bird perches in a pine in Eastern Tennessee. Regarded by old-timers as "the singin'est bird," the mockingbird, (*Mimus Polyglottos*) was chosen by the Tennessee Ornithological Society in April of 1933 to be the state bird.

Cool Water, Fiery Gizzard
BYRON JORJORIAN

Fiery Gizzard Creek feeds the dainty little 12-foot waterfall of Sycamore Falls in the South Cumberland Mountains. Local legend has it that Davy Crockett burned his tongue on a hot chicken gizzard while camping nearby and the name stuck--like a hot, flung gizzard.

(below)

Bat Caves
BYRON JORJORIAN

In 2001 The Nature Conservancy's Tennessee Chapter gained the opportunity to purchase Horseshoe Cliff, in order to protect it from development. 1,541 acres of Cumberland Plateau hardwood forest in the heart of Pickett State Forest, Horseshoe Cliff's many caves are a significant habitat for the èndangered Indiana bat.

(opposite)

Lady's Slipper
BYRON JORJORIAN

Also known as the moccasin flower, the blooms of yellow lady's slipper (*Cypripedium Pubescens*) step out in late spring and early summer.

(above)

**The Grand Canyon
of Tennessee**
BYRON JORJORIAN

The 27,000 acres
flowing through the
Cumberland
Mountains that make
up the Tennessee
River Gorge have
been inhabited by
people for 10,000
years. The meander-
ing Tennessee carves
out diverse land-
forms that provide
habitat for thousands
of native species and
continues to be a life-
line to modern day
Chattanooga.

(opposite)

Valley, My Valley
BYRON JORJORIAN

Early settlers to this
hilly, scenic region on
the Cumberland
Plateau settled in the
fertile mountain val-
leys around Morgan
County. The moun-
tainous terrain and
unnavigable rivers
isolated the region
and slowed settle-
ment. As a result,
farms like this, in
Wartburg, Tennessee
remain seemingly
unchanged.

(above)

Sprawl

BYRON JORJORIAN

Norris Lake was created by a hydro-electric dam on the Clinch and Powell Rivers in 1948. The sprawling lake now covers a vast area on the far eastern edge of the Cumberland Plateau and is a wilderness area that envelops three state recreation areas.

(opposite)

Sha-co-na-ge

BYRON JORJORIAN

The Cherokee word, meaning *The Land of Many Smokes* or *The Land of Blue Mists.* Legend has it that the Cherokee received the gift of fire when the thunders above the sky sent fire down to the mountain and placed it in the heart of a sycamore tree.

Scenic Overlook

BYRON JORJORIAN

Powerful and breathtaking, the forests of the Cumberland Mountains from Frozen Head State Park are, in fact, a series of fragile ecosystems, in danger from air pollution. Also problematic are invasive exotic insects and plants such as honeysuckle and the notorious kudzu vine that can grow up to a foot a day, strangling wide swaths of forest.

**Sunset from Sunset
Point**

BYRON JORJORIAN

Sprawling across
Tennessee and
Kentucky Big South
Fork National River
and Recreation Area is
a wild and remote
area around the
mouth of the Big
South Fork of the
Cumberland River.
The river continues to
carve the gorge's dra-
matic rock formations,
formed by sediments
deposited when the
area was a shallow sea
360 million years ago.

**Buzzard's Wings—
Millikan's Overlook**

BYRON JORJORIAN

Cherokee legend tells
how a great buzzard
formed the mountains
and valleys by press-
ing its wings against
the mud of the earth.

Coming Up Daisies
BYRON JORJORIAN

The Tennessee Wildflower Program has established nearly 800 acres of native wildflowers along interstates and many state routes. The main goals for the 1998 program were to not only enhance the landscape, but also to reduce maintenance costs, increase environmental awareness and propagate and preserve native species. It has become one of the state's most beloved programs.

Lifetime Lease

BYRON JORJORIAN

Settled in 1818, the fertile valley of Cades Cove was a small, farming community deep in the heart of the Smoky Mountains. During the movement to form Great Smoky Mountain Park, many "Cove-ites" resisted the State's cash offers for their land. A compromise allowed them to remain in their homes with a life-time lease. Surrounded by mountain forest, Cades Cove now stands as mute testimony to the tenacity of Tennesseans.

(right)

Winter in Cades Cove

BYRON JORJORIAN

A white tailed buck treads without fear in the empty meadows of Cades Cove in Great Smoky Mountain National Park. The last resident of this isolated rural community, Kermit Caughron died in 1999.

(below)

Roosevelt Drove Through Here

BYRON JORJORIAN

After a long, arduous struggle to create it, President Franklin Roosevelt officially dedicated the Smoky Mountain National Park on September 2nd, 1940. Now recognized as an International Biosphere Reserve and a World Heritage Site. With 9 million visitors annually, it is America's most visited national park.

Un-dammed Wilderness

BYRON JORJORIAN

The Big South Fork River is one of the few rivers in the eastern U.S. that hasn't been dammed. Although majestically beautiful, the vast wilderness through which this untamed river flows is notoriously difficult for human habitation. Native hunters only occasionally ventured into the rocky gorges and forests, but white settlers' permanent homesteads of the early 19th century bore names such as "Difficulty," "Troublesome," and "No Business."

Gone

BYRON JORJORIAN

Many people and cultures have called the Smoky Mountains home and left their mark on the mountains. With their passing from the boundaries of the Smoky Mountains National Park, only animals, plants and memories remain.

(right)

Curiosity
BYRON JORJORIAN

A white tailed deer in Great Smoky Mountain National Park regards visitors. The park's 800 square miles shelters a fabulous diversity of plant and animal life. Scientists have documented 10,000 different species, many of which are found nowhere else on earth. Many believe 90,000 more species may exist in this mountain biosphere.

(below)

Wintering
BYRON JORJORIAN

Winter is quiet in the Smoky Mountain National Park. The blue mists hang over the valleys, dusting the trees with frost. The park focuses on insuring that resident wildlife has enough to survive the winter.

(opposite)

Cold Hearth on a Cold Mountain
BYRON JORJORIAN

Winter comes early in the mountains, with snow falling as early as October or November. The park itself may be a haven of quiet, but in nearby towns such as Gatlinburg, there's skiing, Christmas parades, sleigh rides, craft shows, and other seasonal events to warm the heart.

The Fall of Tradition
BYRON JORJORIAN

An old farm building
stands against another
winter in Williamson,
Tennessee. While
many traditional
farms are giving way
to development in this
fast-growing region,
some farmers opt to
put their land in the
Tennessee Land Trust,
in order to preserve a
vanishing way of life.

Tennessee Pasture
BYRON JORJORIAN

The Tennessee Walk-
ing Horse is a distinc-
tive reflection of both
Tennessee culture and
geography. They are
known for their
smooth ride and sure-
footed gait.

(right)

**Sunshine in
Shady Valley**
BYRON JORJORIAN

Corn harvest in Shady
Valley, in Tennessee's
easternmost county.
Originally the hunting
grounds for Shawnee,
Cherokee, Yuchi and
Creek tribes, this
high valley was
named during the
time when tall hard-
wood forests blocked
the sunlight.

(below)

Lumber Mill
BYRON JORJORIAN

Eastern and Central
Tennessee's wealth of
natural resources
attracted both native
and white settlers for
centuries. Its hard-
wood forests were
vast sources of timber
and abundant rivers
and streams provided
power for mills and
transportation of
commodities to inter-
national markets.

(opposite)

**American Barn
and Silo**
ERNIE PICK

Tennessee's land-
scape attracted a
tough, resilient type
of farmer, notably
Scotch-Irish, German
and English who built
their farm buildings
much like they did in
Europe. Over the cen-
turies, the distinctive
American style
evolved in the rocky
hills and valleys of
Tennessee.

(right)

Rugby Church: A Monument to Utopianism

BYRON JORJORIAN

In 1880, British author and social idealist, Thomas Hughes founded Rugby Colony built on the philosophy of cooperative enterprise and agriculture, culture, and Christian principles. The much-talked about colony both flourished and floundered for ten years before a typhoid epidemic in 1881 began the colony's abrupt decline.

(below)

Rugby Schoolhouse

BYRON JORJORIAN

By 1900 most of the residents of the idyllic Rugby Colony in the Cumberland wilderness had departed for other parts of America. A few residents, including second generation colonists remained to care for the monument to American idealism.

(opposite)

Tennessee Pride

BYRON JORJORIAN

Tennessee's land was not conducive to slavery, and so much of the state had little in common with the interests of the rest of the South. In the events leading up to the American Civil War, Tennessee tried to remain loyal to the Union. It was the last state to join the Confederacy in May 1861.

Granny's Old Homestead

BYRON JORJORIAN

Cades Cove was a tight knit and fiercely self-reliant community. "Cove-ites" depended on neighbors and extended families for survival. By the late 19th century, most of the residents in the isolated Cove were blood relations.

Tobacco Barn

BYRON JORJORIAN

Barns for curing tobacco are a distinctively American invention, but one that varies from region to region. Traditionally, tobacco was a small crop on Tennessee farms and the leaves cured by hanging them from loft poles or roof boards. As tobacco farming increased in the state, specialized curing barns became a regional feature.

Field and Forest

BYRON JORJORIAN

Native cranberry bogs thrived in Tennessee's easternmost region, once heavily forested area until the 1960's when the land was drained for farming. Cranberry bogs are now rare in Johnson County, but are much celebrated during the local October Cranberry Festival.

(above)

A Bridge to the Past
STEVEN SCHMOLDT

American timber and innovation made truss bridges a common feature in Tennessee and elsewhere in the U.S. By 1969, only six remained in Tennessee. Because of their significance and charm, Tennessee works hard to preserve the remaining bridges to the past.

(above)

Corn Crib

BYRON JORJORIAN

Corn was vitally important to early American settlers. Many small barns in the Tennessee mountains, such as this early log barn in Cades Cove, may have first been the main dwelling and then later served as a corncrib.

(above)

Fire in the Sky
BYRON JORJORIAN

The sun over the Great Smoky Mountains changes the mist to a fiery orange. A Cherokee legend tells of a witch named Spearfinger, who lived on the crest of mountains and hid in the mist.

(above)

Smoke Rising

BYRON JORJORIAN

The smoke of the Smoky Mountains, caused by natural oils and water vapor released by plants, rises from hollows and coves, veiling the autumn mountains in mystery. It was into these rugged mountains that many Cherokee fled from Federal soldiers to escape their forcible removal in 1838. Many struggled to survive the mountain winters.

Night time in Chattanooga

BYRON JORJORIAN

Chattanooga's name is derived from the Creek Indian word meaning "rock that comes to a point". The Valley around the Tennessee River was the last capital of the Cherokee Nation. As an important railroad center for the South, in 1863, it was the strategic site of The Battle of Chickamauga and the Battle of Chattanooga, two of the bloodiest battles in the Civil War. Since then, the "Scenic City," at the base of the Blue Ridge, is one of the South's most popular tourist sites.

Walking on Walnut Street

BYRON JORJORIAN

The Walnut Street Pedestrian Bridge in Chattanooga seems to take its inspiration from the city's railroading history. Established in 1839, Chattanooga's geography made it a strategic junction for river traffic and the arrival of the railroad in 1849. Chattanooga boomed during railroading heyday.

Freshwater Perspective
BYRON JORJORIAN

145,000 square feet, five levels including two living forests and a dramatic canyon, and 575 different species make Tennessee Aquarium in Chattanooga the world's largest freshwater aquarium. Opened in May 1992, the distinctive building on the banks of the Tennessee River spotlights native river ecosystems, but boasts freshwater fish and their habitats around the world. The $45 million facility has recently been slated for expansion.

Contributors

Louisa Avery
7544 Rolling River Parkway
Nashville, TN 37221

Randy Lynn Blevins
P.O. Box 100903
Nashville, TN 37224-0903

Anne Bond
4322 Glen Eden Drive
Nashville, TN 37205

Bob Guthridge
2994 Leyland Cove
Memphis, TN 38119

Thomas "Hank" Hogan
411 S. Central Street
Clarksville, AR 72830

Monty Johnson
1617 Faxon
Memphis, TN 38112

Byron Jorjorian Photography
PO Box 306
Thompson Station, TN 37179
byron@naturephotocentral.com

Khena Kara
1608 MapleTimber Court
Antioch, TN 37013

Gary Kessel
11223 Barbara Cove
Eads, TN 38028

Steve Morgan
2024 Lakefront Drive Apt.20
Collerville, TN 38017

Ernest Pick
4012 Bonita Avenue
Coconut Grove, FL 33133

Charles Reist
1613 Livingstone Street
Sarasota, FL. 34231-6619

Steven Schmoldt
117 Bakertown Road
Antioch, TN 37013-5050

Mindy Schwartz
400 Longhunter Court
Nashville, TN 37217

Kandie Strefling
1524 E 53rd Street
Savannah, GA 31404

Country Music Hall of Fame

Gaylord Opryland Resort and
Convention Center

Memphis Convention and
Visitors Bureau

Peabody Hotel